6/09

20,95

# The Maryland Colony: Lord Baltimore

Mitchell Lane
PUBLISHERS

P.O. Box 196 • Hockessin, Delaware 19707

# Titles in the Series

# The Maryland Colony:
# Lord Baltimore

Jim Whiting

Copyright © 2008 by Mitchell Lane Publishers, Inc. All rights reserved. No part of this book may be reproduced without written permission from the publisher. Printed and bound in the United States of America.

Printing     1       2       3       4       5       6       7       8       9

Library of Congress Cataloging-in-Publication Data
Whiting, Jim, 1943–
    The Maryland Colony : Lord Baltimore / by Jim Whiting.
       p. cm. — (Building America)
    Includes bibliographical references and index.
    Audience: Grades 7-8.
    ISBN 978-1-58415-547-8 (library bound : alk. paper)
    1. Maryland—History—Colonial period, ca. 1600–1775—Juvenile literature. 2. Baltimore, Charles Calvert, Lord, 1637–1715—Juvenile literature. 3. Calvert family—Juvenile literature. 4. Maryland—History—1775–1865—Juvenile literature. I. Title.
F184.W495 2008
975.2'02—dc22
                                                                                    2007023413

ABOUT THE AUTHOR: Jim Whiting has been a remarkably versatile and accomplished journalist, writer, editor, and photographer for more than 30 years. He has read widely in American colonial history and events leading up to the emergence of the new nation. A voracious reader since early childhood, Mr. Whiting has written and edited more than 250 nonfiction children's books on a wide range of topics. He lives in Washington state with his wife and two teenage sons.

ON THE COVER: Leonard Calvert plants a cross to mark the first settlement of Maryland Colony.

PHOTO CREDITS: Cover, pp. 1, 3, 6, 14, 16, 22, 30, 37—North Wind Picture Archives; p. 12—painting by Hans the Younger Holbein; p. 13—painting by Isaac Oliver; p. 17—Faith Rowland; p. 18—painting by Gerard Soest; p. 21—painting by Louis Glanzman; p. 25—Annapolis & Anne Arundel County; p. 27—painting by Justus Engelhardt Kühn; p. 28, 33—Jonathan Scott; p. 31—Library of Congress; p. 34—painting by Allan Ramsay; p. 38—National Atlas of the United States; p. 40—painting by Emanuel Leutze.

PUBLISHER'S NOTE: This story is based on the author's extensive research, which he believes to be accurate. Documentation of such research is contained on page 46. The internet sites referenced herein were active as of the publication date. Due to the fleeting nature of some web sites, we cannot guarantee they will all be active when you are reading this book.

                                                                                    PLB

# Contents

*For Your Information

*George Calvert radiates confidence in a portrait that probably dates to about 1620. Soon he would be named the Baron of Baltimore and launch a program of colonization that began in Newfoundland, Canada. Finding the cold climate there did not suit him, he obtained a royal grant to establish the more temperate Maryland Colony.*

## Chapter

# Sailing to "Mary's Land"

As the *Ark* repeatedly rose, dropped, and shuddered on the icy November ocean, the passengers grew more terrified. "Such a tempest broke forth towards evening, that it seemed that we would be enveloped by the waves with every motion," wrote passenger Andrew White. "Everyone was hastening to purify his soul through the Sacrament of Penance; for when we had lost control over the rudder, the vessel, abandoned to the waves and winds, soon tossed about like a quoit [game piece]."[1]

Despite the passengers' fears, the *Ark*, headed from England to the New World, was not destined for destruction. "God opened a path for her safety,"[2] noted White, who was a Catholic priest. In his eyes the voyage had religious purposes: "to honor the blood of our Redeemer through the salvation of the savages, [and] to erect a kingdom for the Savior."[3]

The "kingdom" lay nearly 3,000 miles away in the New World, where passengers aboard the *Ark* and a smaller ship, the *Dove*, planned to establish a new colony. The roots of the voyage had taken hold more than a century earlier during the reign of King Henry VIII, when a religious conflict began in England. The conflict was between the Catholic Church and the Church of England (which practiced the Protestant religion called Anglicism). The turmoil played an important role in the life of George Calvert, an English nobleman who spearheaded the expedition.

Born in 1580, Calvert was raised in Yorkshire. According to the Church of England, Yorkshire was a region in which every gentleman was "evil in religion"[4]—that is, Catholic. In 1592, authorities discovered that young Calvert was learning from a "popish primer"[5]—a schoolbook based on the tenets of Catholicism. George's father, Leonard Calvert, was ordered to conform to the official English religion of Anglicism and to send his sons to a Protestant tutor.

As a result, George Calvert appeared to have accepted Anglicism when he joined the court of the new English king, James I, in 1603. He immediately found a mentor at court: Sir Robert Cecil, the king's most trusted adviser. Calvert became one of Cecil's secretaries and swiftly rose in importance. When Calvert's wife gave birth to their first son in 1605, he named the little boy Cecilius after his patron.

Calvert became interested in the New World in 1609 when he invested in the Virginia Company, which had established the Jamestown Colony two years earlier. It was the first English settlement in the New World. If he had any Catholic sympathies, he kept them well hidden, for anyone even suspected of being a Catholic couldn't participate in the venture. The following year he invested in the East India Company, another business looking to make profits in the New World.

These and other enterprises made Calvert a wealthy man. In 1619, when he was appointed as one of two secretaries of state, he became one of the most powerful men in England. In 1624, however, he fell from power when he failed to negotiate a marriage between James's son and a Spanish princess. Early in 1625, he resigned his position as secretary of state and declared that he was embracing Catholicism. No one knows if this conversion to his original faith was sudden or an acknowledgement that Calvert had secretly practiced Catholicism all along.

Despite Calvert's declaration, the king didn't bear him any ill will. In 1623, James had given him an estate in Ireland, the Manor of Baltimore. Now the king bestowed the title of Baron of Baltimore on him. From then on, Calvert would also be known as Lord Baltimore.

His departure from court enabled him to devote his full attention to the colony in Newfoundland (in what is now Canada) he had established in 1621. He believed that a combination of farming and fishing would make it profitable and support a steadily growing population. Reports that had filtered back to him in the succeeding years had been promising. In the summer of 1627, he paid a brief visit to the colony for a firsthand look. While disappointed at the slow rate of colonization, he returned the following year with most of his family and at least thirty settlers, fully intending to settle in for a long stay.

He quickly became disenchanted with the colony. One reason was that the French had already established a foothold in the region and resented any newcomers. He had to devote time and energy to fighting off French attacks on his fishing vessels.

He expressed another reason in a letter to the new king, Charles I: "From the midst of October to the midst of May, there is a sad face of winter upon all this land, both sea and land so frozen as they are not penetrable, no plant or vegetable thing appearing out of the earth until it be about the beginning of May."[6] His home became a virtual hospital, with dozens of ill colonists coming in and out. Several died, and the harsh conditions adversely affected his own health.

Calvert was certainly discouraged. Yet he had an "inclination carrying me naturally to these kind of works [colonization], and not knowing how to better employ the poor remainder of my days,"[7] he confidently assured the king that he would continue to further English settlement in the New World. He asked the king for a new charter, in the Chesapeake Bay region adjacent to the colony at Jamestown. Unwilling to endure another Newfoundland winter while waiting for the king's reply, Calvert bundled up his family and most of the colonists and set sail for Virginia.

He encountered a rude reception. The Virginians not only didn't want to share what they regarded as their own territory, but they also deeply resented his Catholicism. They ordered him to leave. In a somewhat congratulatory letter to the king, they boasted that "no papists [Catholics] have been suffered to settle their abode among us."[8]

Calvert sailed for England, leaving his wife behind. The Virginians' rebuff strengthened his resolve to establish a colony where

Catholics would be welcome. His one success in Newfoundland had been to create conditions in which Protestants and Catholics could coexist in peace—a rarity in that era.

He spent the next few years trying to convince the king to give him the land he desired. It was a difficult task. The king was under intense pressure from the Virginians, who remained violently opposed to having Calvert as a neighbor. It didn't help that Calvert's health, weakened by his stay in Newfoundland, was steadily declining. He was also saddened by the death of his wife, who drowned in a shipwreck as she was returning to England.

Calvert persevered, and early in 1632 the king granted him nearly seven million acres in the upper reaches of Chesapeake Bay north of the Potomac River. The northern boundary was fixed at the fortieth parallel, which would later cause many problems. The grant also gave Calvert sweeping powers. As historian Aubrey Lord notes: "The Baron of Baltimore was truly Lord Proprietor, actual owner of the soil and sovereign in government, subject only to his allegiance to the King."[9] Calvert would be a virtual king in his dominions. One advantage of this situation was that he could establish his own policy toward religion.

At first Calvert wanted to call his grant Crescentia. Charles had other ideas. He wanted it named Terra Maria, to honor his wife, Henrietta Mary, herself a Catholic. The colony thus became Land Maria, or Mary's Land.

Weakened by his exertions, Calvert died several weeks before the grant became official. His two eldest sons, Cecilius and Leonard, both in their mid-twenties, took over the plans for colonization. Cecilius, as the older son, became the second Lord Baltimore and first proprietor of Maryland. He would remain in England to handle the administrative details and make sure that the Virginians didn't scuttle their efforts. Leonard would head up the actual expedition and become the first governor. Andrew White, who had met George Calvert sometime during the previous few years, helped out by writing a promotional tract, "Declaratio Coloniae Domini Baronis de Baltimore," in an effort to attract settlers.

While Cecilius Calvert saw his new holding as a way of providing protection for Catholics, he also made it clear that making money was the most important thing. The best way of insuring a profit was to eliminate any sources of religious strife. He told Leonard to "cause all Acts of the Romane Catholique Religion to be done as privately as may be and . . . [to] instruct all the Roman Catholiques to be silent upon [all] occasions of discourse concerning matters of Religion."[10]

The *Dove* and the *Ark* left England with perhaps 150 people on board. While a few were sons of Catholic landowners, the rest were Protestants. Some were indentured servants, while others were farmers and men with skills that would be valuable in the new colony.

Late November wasn't the ideal time to cross the Atlantic Ocean, but if the colonists left then, they would arrive in the New World in early spring. The settlers could begin planting the crops that would sustain them. Almost immediately the ships ran into the rough weather that White documented. When it passed, the colonists enjoyed excellent weather for the remainder of the voyage. After stopping over at the Caribbean island of Barbados, the two vessels entered Chesapeake Bay in early March.

White chronicled his first impressions in the *Relatio Itineris in Marilandia* (Voyage to Maryland), which was rushed into print as a supplement to his earlier work and to serve as a further inducement to settle in Maryland. He was especially impressed with the Potomac River. "You will hardly find a more pleasant, evenly flowing river," he wrote. "Compared with it, the Thames [a major river in England] seems a mere rivulet. It is not tainted by swamps, but on both sides wonderful forests of fine trees rise up on solid ground, not made inaccessible by thorn hedges and underbrush, but just as if planted spaciously by hand so that one could easily drive a chariot drawn by four horses between the trees."[11] He also noted an abundance of fish and game, plenty of fresh water, rich soil, a profusion of wild berries and nuts—in short, virtually ideal physical conditions.

The colonists went ashore on St. Clement's Island. On March 25, 1634, White led them in their first mass of thanksgiving. It was an auspicious date, the Feast of the Annunciation, the first day of the new

*King Charles I, who reigned from 1625 to 1649, granted George Calvert a colony next to Virginia. The colony was called Maryland after Charles' wife, Henrietta Mary.*

year in terms of the calendar then in use. In schools and offices across the state, March 25 is still celebrated as Maryland Day.

Although the landing went smoothly, there was still one very large area of uncertainty: the attitude of the local Indians. The colonists were fully aware of the problems that the Jamestown settlers had had in establishing their colony. These problems had culminated in 1622 with an Indian uprising that resulted in the death of hundreds of Virginians.

Luck was on their side. Aided by Henry Fleet, a Virginian who became friendly with the local Indians and was fluent in their languages, helped the colonists let the Yaocomico, the local tribe, know that they came in peace. The Yaocomico were willing to deal with the newcomers. White wrote: "We bought thirty miles of that land from the chieftain in exchange for hatchets, axes, hoes, rakes, and some amount of cloth."[12]

It was an astounding bargain. The colonists not only acquired an extensive parcel of land—which they named St. Mary—but the departing Yaocomico also gave them their houses and fields, which were already prepared for spring planting. As a result, the new Marylanders were able to settle in right away and raise enough corn to satisfy their own needs, with a little extra for export. They also began planting tobacco, the primary cash crop of Virginia and one reason George Calvert had wanted to establish his colony next door. White concluded, "This is the finger of God."[13]

But even in this apparent Eden, problems were about to arise.

## Religious Strife in England

When Henry VIII became king of England in 1509, there were no divisions in the Christian Church. That changed in 1517 when German clergyman Martin Luther began the Protestant Reformation. At first, Henry opposed Luther, and Pope Leo X praised Henry as a "defender of the faith."

Soon after becoming king, Henry married Katherine, a Spanish princess. They had a daughter, Mary, who would be their only child. Henry, who desperately wanted a male heir, decided to divorce Katherine and marry Anne Boleyn, hoping Anne would bear him a son. Because the Church forbade divorce, Henry asked the pope to make an exception for him. The pope refused.

Henry decided to start his own church—the Anglican Church, or Church of England—which would allow divorces. It was definitely Protestant. While many people joined the new church, some Catholics refused. Religious conflict in England began.

Anne disappointed Henry by giving birth to a daughter, Elizabeth. Later Henry thought she was cheating on him so he executed her. His third wife, Jane Seymour, gave him a son, Edward, who was never in good health. Edward became king in 1547 but died six years later. Mary succeeded him and reestablished the Catholic faith in England. She was nicknamed "Bloody Mary" because she ordered the burning of thousands of Protestants.

When Mary died in 1558, Elizabeth became queen and restored her father's church. The English Parliament passed anti-Catholic laws. Many Catholics continued to practice their religion in secret and hoped to overthrow Elizabeth. Catholic Spain tried to help by sending the Spanish Armada against England in 1588. The attempt failed.

Catholics weren't Elizabeth's only religious problem. She also had to deal with Puritans, who believed in a much purer and simpler form of worship.

Elizabeth's death in 1603 didn't end these conflicts. A group of dissatisfied Catholics organized the Gunpowder Plot in 1605 in an effort to blow up King James I. Its failure resulted in more anti-Catholic laws. Meanwhile, the Puritans continued to pressure James to give them a greater role in government.

Queen Elizabeth I,
*The Rainbow Portrait,*
1600, by Isaac Oliver

For Your Information

*The trading post on Kent Island in Chesapeake Bay was established by Virginia settler William Claiborne. He soon came into conflict with the Calverts because Kent Island was part of their grant from Charles I. He eventually lost control of the island and spent many years trying to regain it. He finally retired from politics in 1660 and spent the last years of his life managing his estate in Virginia.*

Chapter

## Conflicts Begin

The English—and other Europeans—were accustomed to conflicts as they began establishing colonies in North America. Almost always these conflicts were with the Indians, the original inhabitants who resisted the encroachments on their lands.

Initially, the Marylanders had little reason to expect anything different. "We were keeping watch night and day, to protect at one time our woodcutters against sudden attacks,"[1] White had written. Building a fort to protect themselves had been one of the top priorities when they came ashore. When it became obvious that the Yaocomico and other tribes didn't pose a threat, they tore it down. White and the other priests soon busied themselves with the task of bringing Christianity to the Indians, whom they considered "savages." White learned how to speak the native languages, compiled a dictionary, and wrote a grammar book.

The first conflict in Maryland actually came from an unexpected direction: another Englishman. William Claiborne came to Virginia in 1621 and quickly rose to prominence. Several years later he began exploring the northern reaches of Chesapeake Bay and established a fur trading enterprise with the Indians. He was a leader of the opposition to George Calvert, even making the long voyage to England in an effort to thwart Calvert's grant. In 1631 he set up a permanent base on Kent Island, which lay in the territory the king later granted to Calvert.

When Leonard Calvert and the rest of the colonists landed, Claiborne refused to accept their authority. He said that the king's charter only applied to uncultivated land. His settlement—which included a church, store, several houses, and cleared ground—was definitely cultivated and therefore belonged to him and not the Calverts.

There was probably another factor at work. As historian Robert J. Brugger explains, "[Claiborne] typified the swashbucklers that English ambition of the day sprouted in foreign parts. Proud, impulsive, and untamed, he sought out adventure and loved a good fight."[2]

It didn't take long for "a good fight" to erupt. Early in 1635, Claiborne's agents seized one of Calvert's trading vessels. Calvert forces retaliated by capturing the *Long Tayle*, which belonged to Claiborne.

*Some historians consider the Battle of Pocomoke Sound, the fight between two of Calvert's boats and one belonging to Claiborne, as the first naval battle in the future United States. The Calvert boats won, nearly sinking Claiborne's vessel.*

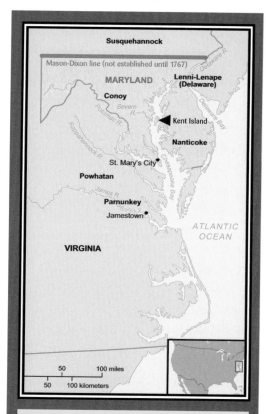

Susquehannock

Mason-Dixon line (not established until 1767)

MARYLAND      Lenni-Lenape
                   (Delaware)
Conoy

Kent Island

Nanticoke

St. Mary's City

Powhatan

Parnunkey

Jamestown

ATLANTIC
OCEAN

VIRGINIA

50      100 miles

50      100 kilometers

*The chief settlements of the Maryland and Virginia colonies were Jamestown and St. Mary's City. Kent Island, originally settled by a Virginian, was later granted as part of the Maryland Colony. Main Indian groups in the region are also shown. The northern Chesapeake Bay tributary, the Susquehanna River, was named by the Susquehannock.*

On April 23, Claiborne's boat *Cockatrice*—commanded by Ratcliffe Warren—spotted the *St. Helen,* a Calvert vessel. Warren planned to sneak up on the *St. Helen,* swarm aboard with his men, and capture it before the stunned crew could fight back. Though the sudden appearance of another Calvert vessel, the *St. Margaret,* scuttled that approach, Warren didn't back down and attacked both vessels. During the ensuing combat (which some historians consider the first naval combat in the future United States) Warren and two other *Cockatrice* crewmen were killed. The vessel itself was badly damaged and nearly sank.

There was an immediate aftereffect. With an English civil war looming and threatening to disrupt the fur trade, the London-based company that sold Claiborne's furs in Europe replaced Claiborne with another man. This replacement, George Evelin, was willing to accept the authority of the Calverts. By 1638, the Calverts had established their authority over Kent Island.

Claiborne was far from finished. He would continue to be a thorn in the side of the Calverts for many years.

*Cecilius Calvert, as portrayed by Gerard Soest, court painter to King Charles II, 1670. Calvert holds a map of Maryland, which he had printed more than thirty years earlier. The child clutching the map is his grandson Cecil. The little boy would have become Lord Baltimore but died in 1681. The other boy is their attendant.*

The year 1638 was significant for another reason. An assembly representing all the colony's freemen had met for the first time three years earlier and drafted a number of "wholesome lawes and ordinances then made and provided for the welfare of this Province."[3]

Cecilius Calvert didn't like the idea that anyone other than he could establish laws. He replied, "We do disassent unto all the laws by [the Assembly] heretofore or at any time made within our said Province, and do declare them to be void."[4] He sent the Assembly a copy of the laws that he wanted to be used in governing the colony, fully expecting the members to either accept them outright or suggest relatively minor changes.

The Assembly balked. It not only voted against accepting the laws, but went a step further and drew up yet another set of laws. Its members believed that they were in a better position to develop laws because they knew the actual conditions that existed in the colony, while Calvert was 3,000 miles away. In the end, the two sides accepted a compromise. The Assembly passed forty-three acts: twenty-six were theirs, and the other seventeen were Baltimore's. The Assembly had also made its point: It had the right to initiate legislation.

This spirit of compromise would have been useful for the king. Even before his grant to George Calvert, Charles had been feuding with Parliament. He refused to compromise, and the feuding broke out into civil war in 1642. The leader of the rebellion was a Puritan named Oliver Cromwell, and many other Puritans played leading roles.

The ripples of the rebellion spread to Maryland. A Puritan ship captain named Richard Ingle invaded the colony early in 1645. Leonard Calvert and many settlers fled to Virginia. Ingle imprisoned White and the other Catholic priests and controlled the colony for nearly two years, until Calvert recruited some soldiers in Virginia and reclaimed the colony. Calvert died a few months later. One of the most remarkable women in early American colonial history, Margaret Brent, was named the executor of his will. She had to figure out how to use his estate to pay the troops who had recaptured the colony.

Even though Ingle was gone, the Puritan influence remained. The Puritans in England had won the civil war and imprisoned Charles. Baltimore wanted to keep a low religious profile—the Puritans were no friends of the Catholics—so in 1649 he appointed a Protestant named William Stone as the colony's new governor. Stone immediately extended an invitation to some 300 Puritans in Virginia—who found themselves unwelcome there—to come to Maryland and receive land plus full civil rights. The new arrivals founded the town of Providence.

At the same time, Stone urged the Assembly to pass an "Act Concerning Religion." It not only mandated heavy penalties for making negative comments about anyone's religion, it also stipulated that "no person or persons whatsoever within this Province . . . professing to believe in Jesus Christ, shall from henceforth be any way troubled, molested, or discountenanced for or in respect of his or her religion nor in the free exercise thereof."[5]

Also known as the Toleration Act, it was the first legislation for religious freedom in the English-speaking world. Ironically, it was passed at about the same time that the Puritans executed King Charles.

The Puritans themselves proved to be somewhat intolerant. In 1654, with the aid of William Claiborne, they took over the colony's government. They quickly repealed the Toleration Act and forbade Catholics to practice their faith. Three years later, they relinquished control, restored the Toleration Act, and recognized Calvert's authority as the proprietor. Following a brief upheaval in 1660, which Calvert called the "pygmy rebellion" because of its relative unimportance, Calvert's "time of troubles" came to an end. At the same time, Charles II—the son of Charles I—restored the English monarchy.

Cecilius Calvert died in 1675. During more than forty years of owning the charter, he never saw his colony. His son Charles succeeded him as the third Lord Baltimore and proprietor of Maryland. As his father had had problems with Virginia to the south, Charles Calvert would soon have his own conflict, this time to the north.

In 1681, King Charles II gave William Penn a huge tract of land in North America, which was named Pennsylvania. The southern boundary of Pennsylvania was set at the fortieth parallel—the northern border of Maryland. Penn quickly sent colonists to begin settling his new domain, and they established Philadelphia as the capital before making an accurate determination of where the boundary line actually lay. As a result, the site of Philadelphia was below the fortieth parallel, technically making it part of Maryland. In addition, Penn wanted three counties on the Delaware Peninsula, the land that lay between the Atlantic Ocean and the Chesapeake Bay. Though these counties were clearly within the original Calvert charter, Penn needed them to give Philadelphia an outlet to the sea.

The king sent a letter to Calvert ordering him to meet with Penn and "make a true division and separation"[6] of their respective provinces. Meetings between the two men, who didn't get along, didn't solve anything. Penn suggested that the king really didn't mean to establish the border at the fortieth parallel, but rather the thirty-ninth. Calvert rejected the idea. The dispute grew serious enough that both men sailed to England in 1684 to plead their respective cases before the king. Charles Calvert would never return to Maryland.

## Margaret Brent

Born in 1601, Margaret Brent came to Maryland in 1638 with her sister and two brothers. Neither Margaret nor her sister was married, and they remained single for the rest of their lives.

Margaret became a landowner, lent money to new colonists, conducted business in court, and took part in other activities that she couldn't have done had she been married. She may even have saved the colony after Richard Ingle had been expelled. The men who helped Leonard Calvert retake Maryland demanded the money he had promised to pay them. When he died, there wasn't enough money in his estate to meet the soldiers' financial demands, and they became unruly. Maryland teetered on the brink of chaos.

Margaret was in the middle of the problem, as Calvert had appointed her executor of his estate. She wanted to raise taxes to complete the payoff, so she addressed the Assembly and demanded two votes: one for herself as a landowner and the other as Leonard Calvert's attorney. At that time, women didn't have the right to vote. The members turned her down and refused to consider measures that might have satisfied the soldiers. Margaret found another solution. She sold cattle belonging to Lord Baltimore to repay them.

Back in London, Baltimore was furious about the loss of his family's cattle. The Assembly wrote him in support of Margaret. "We do Verily Believe that [your estate] was better for the Collonys safety at that time in her hands then in any mans else," the members said, "for the Soldiers would never have treated any other with . . . Civility and respect. . . . She rather deserved favour and thanks from your Honour for her so much Concurring to the publick safety."[7] Calvert ignored the Assembly's words and remained angry with Margaret. Under this pressure, she left Maryland about 1651 and resettled in Virginia in an estate she named Peace, where she lived a prosperous life until her death twenty years later.

Margaret Brent addressing the Assembly

*A gentleman takes his ease while smoking a pipe filled with "Old Maryland" tobacco. Tobacco purchases by many men like him formed a vital part of Maryland's economy.*

Chapter

# 3

## Protestants Come to Power

In 1685, the English Board of Trade and Plantations awarded the eastern half of the Delaware peninsula north of a certain point to Penn (nearly a century later, this portion broke away and became the Delaware Colony). It reaffirmed that the border between Maryland and Pennsylvania would remain at the fortieth parallel, though the decision was soon amended to place the dividing line nineteen miles south of the parallel. The change would allow Philadelphia to remain in Pennsylvania.

Meanwhile, England was going through another political crisis. Charles II died early in 1685, and his brother James II succeeded him. James had three major strikes against him: He was a Catholic, he appointed Catholics to important political offices, and—like his father, Charles I—he tried to rule in an almost dictatorial fashion. Three years later, he was deposed in what became known as the Glorious Revolution. His Protestant daughter Mary and her husband, William, assumed the throne.

Once again, English politics had an influence on Maryland. Charles Calvert had become increasingly unpopular during his final years there. Virtually all of his appointments went to Catholics or Protestants who had married into his family. At the same time, Catholics in general were doing better economically than Protestants, who resented their success. Charles Calvert's nephew George Talbot, the acting governor, stabbed a royal tax collector to death. Talbot's replacement as governor, a Catholic named William Joseph, said that power in the colony originated with God, who in turn gave it "to the King, and from the King to his Excellency the lord Proprietor [Calvert], and from his said Lordship to Us."[1] The statement seemed to indicate that the Calverts and their allies could do what they wanted. There were even rumors that the colony's Catholics were planning to ally themselves with local Indians in order to massacre the Protestants.

Inspired by the events in England, the following summer, 1686, a group of Maryland's leading Protestants—who called themselves the Protestant Association—pledged to "pressure, vindicate and assert the Sovereign Dominion and right of King William and Queen Mary to this Province; to defend the Protestant Religion among us and to protect and shelter the Inhabitants from all manner of violence, oppression and destruction that is plotted and designed against them."[2] This pledge attracted enough support to allow the Protestant Association to take over the government in a bloodless revolution. They asked the new monarchs to take away the Calverts' authority and replace it with their own. For the next twenty-five years, Maryland would be under the direct control of the English crown.

An "Act of Religion" extended the penal laws of England to Maryland. As a result, Maryland could officially discriminate against Catholics, and the government took away many of their rights.

Lionel Copley, the first royal governor, arrived in 1692. He died soon afterward and was replaced by Francis Nicholson. Nicholson wanted to move the colony's capital from St. Mary, with its close association with the Calverts. He chose Annapolis (named in honor of Princess Anne, who would become Queen Anne in 1702). Annapolis has remained the capital of Maryland ever since.

Nicholson was an especially energetic governor. He laid out the streets of Annapolis, was instrumental in founding King William's School in 1696 (the first school in Maryland supported by public

*King William's School became St. John's College in 1784. Today St. John's is a private college with just under 500 students. It is especially noted for its Great Books program. The campus is across the street from the U.S. Naval Academy, and the two schools have an annual croquet match. St. John's almost always wins.*

funds), and established the Anglican Church as the official church of Maryland. Catholics were forbidden to hold public office or to celebrate public masses.

They weren't the only ones affected by the Glorious Revolution. From the time of the first landing and for several decades afterward, Maryland tobacco planters used primarily indentured white servants to work in their fields. Slavery developed relatively slowly until Maryland legalized the practice in 1663. Then slavers began bringing in African people by the hundreds. The number of slaves in Maryland nearly tripled between 1697 and 1710. Numbering around 8,000, they composed nearly 20 percent of the colony's population. Within 50 years, nearly half of all Maryland planters would own slaves.

As more slaves were brought into the colony, the pace of immigration from England also picked up. One of these immigrants was eighteen-year-old Daniel Dulany. Hardly anyone besides his two brothers, who also made the passage in 1703, paid any attention to him. By the time of his death, he was extremely wealthy, and his name had become virtually a household word. His success was an example of why so many people came to Maryland.

Queen Anne died in 1714 and was succeeded by George I. At the same time, the Calverts—who still owned millions of unsettled acres—enjoyed a return to power. To the immense displeasure of his father, Benedict Leonard Calvert had renounced Catholicism. Now a Protestant and freed from the colony's anti-Catholic laws, he asked to have colonial authority returned to his family. When his father died in February 1715, he became the fourth Lord Baltimore and third proprietor. Within two months he was dead. His son Charles, who had also renounced Catholicism, succeeded him. Reflecting the changing conditions in the colony, neither man had the same powers as his predecessors.

Other conditions were changing as well. While tobacco remained important to the colony's economy, some planters were emphasizing crops such as corn and wheat and exporting much of what they grew. They also raised livestock and sold it to the West Indies.

Growers were particularly interested in the swift-flowing rivers that fed into the western side of Chesapeake Bay because the water powered the mills that ground the grain. One such river was the Patapsco, which ended in a large sheltered cove where ships could tie up and take on the freshly milled flour. The provincial government established a customs house there in 1729, and a village named Baltimore grew up around it. Though its growth was slow in its early decades, in time Baltimore would become by far the largest city in Maryland and among the most populous in the entire United States.

## A Rags-to-Riches Story

What historian Carl Bode terms "the story of one man who more than any other symbolized the history of Maryland as a colony"[3] began in 1703 with the arrival of eighteen-year-old Daniel Dulany. Dulany was a redemptioner: With no money to pay for his passage, the ship's captain would sell Dulany's services to a wealthy planter to cover the cost of his fare.

In Dulany's case, the planter was Colonel George Plater II. Bode explains, "Dulany received his training there in the two areas most important to an ambitious young Marylander, law and tobacco farming."[4] Dulany completed his obligation to Plater in 1709 and opened his own law office. A year later he earned a well-paid appointment as a clerk of the court. Within a few years, he had purchased several tracts of land. He hinted that he was destined for success when he had his portrait painted—something that was relatively expensive. Soon afterward he married into one of the colony's most notable families.

By 1720 he had amassed 27,000 acres, making him one of Maryland's largest landowners. He cemented his growing reputation and importance by building one of the largest mansions in Annapolis. Shortly afterward he became the colony's attorney general. Other political offices soon followed.

By the end of the decade he had acquired another title: landlord. He bought property, rented it at low rates—often taking his payment in crops rather than money—then sold the property at a profit after his tenants had improved it.

A similar strategy in 1730 became especially lucrative. Dulany acquired territory in western Maryland, far from the water outlets that tobacco farmers needed to ship their products and therefore ignored by most land speculators. Dulany bought large tracts and then sold them in small allotments. He had so many buyers that he needed to found a town to serve them. He named it Frederick, after the current Lord Baltimore's son. Today Frederick is Maryland's second largest city.

Dulany died in 1753 as one of the colony's wealthiest and most respected citizens—exactly fifty years after his arrival with little more than the shirt on his back.

Portrait of Daniel Dulany

FYI

★ For Your Information ★

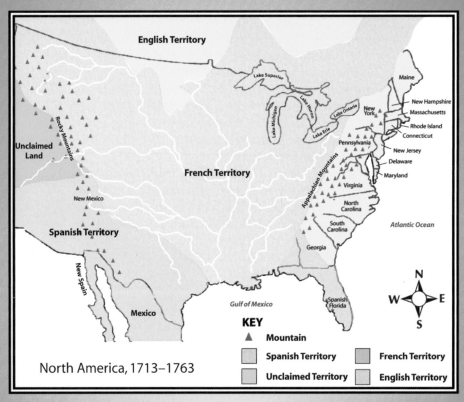

**English Territory**

Lake Superior

Maine

Lake Huron

Lake Ontario

New Hampshire

Lake Michigan

Lake Erie

Massachusetts

New York

Rhode Island

Connecticut

Pennsylvania

New Jersey

Rocky Mountains

Unclaimed Land

Delaware

Maryland

**French Territory**

Appalachian Mountains

Virginia

New Mexico

North Carolina

**Spanish Territory**

South Carolina

Atlantic Ocean

Georgia

New Spain

Spanish Florida

Gulf of Mexico

Mexico

N
W    E
S

**KEY**

▲ Mountain

☐ Spanish Territory          ☐ French Territory

☐ Unclaimed Territory        ☐ English Territory

North America, 1713–1763

By 1763, England, France, and Spain held claims in North America. When the French built a fort in western Virginia, the British colonists retaliated, sending George Washington to defend the territory. Maryland Colony also supported Washington in these frontier battles, which marked the beginning of the French and Indian War.

Chapter

4

## Drawing the Line

As Maryland became ever more prosperous, a more precise definition of the border with Pennsylvania had to be made. In spite of the 1685 judgment, the line had never been firmly established. The Calverts had encouraged settlement in the region that both Maryland and Pennsylvania claimed, sometimes even knowingly above the fortieth parallel. The situation came to a head in the 1730s in what became known as the Conojacular Wars, which involved raids conducted by both sides and centered around a Maryland man named Thomas Cresap. Cresap, who came to Maryland at the age of fifteen, was known as the Maryland Monster because of his role in attacks on Pennsylvanians. He enjoyed the full support of his wife, who, according to historian Robert J. Brugger, "carried a rifle, two pistols, a tomahawk, a scalping knife, and, in her boot, a small dagger."[1]

Cresap shot and killed a Pennsylvania deputy who tried to arrest him in 1734. Two years later, a posse succeeded in taking him into custody. When he arrived in Philadelphia, he defiantly said: "This is one of the prettiest towns in Maryland."[2] Cresap became a legendary figure in Maryland, aided by the claim that he now has more than 11,000 descendants. But not even his capture could end the boundary controversy. It continued to drag on, though not as violently as before.

In the early days of the Maryland Colony, indentured servants worked the tobacco fields. Within decades, they were largely replaced by African slaves.

By the early 1750s, the colonists were moving away from the original settlements on the Chesapeake and heading inland. A census taken in 1755 revealed Maryland's growth. The population was slightly over 150,000. About 28 percent of it, or nearly 43,000, were slaves. In prime tobacco-growing regions, slaves sometimes exceeded 50 percent of the population.

When this census was taken, a cloud hung over the colony. Just over a century after the brief overthrow of the Calvert government by the Puritans, Maryland was threatened again. This time the danger came from the west rather than from overseas.

For decades, the English and French had been rivals for control of the North American heartland. In 1754, the French built Fort Duquesne at the forks of the Ohio River, in land claimed by Virginia. A few months later, Virginia troops led by Lieutenant Colonel George Washington fought a skirmish with the French. Then Washington was attacked by a much larger body of troops and compelled to surrender.

The victorious French allowed him to leave the scene of the battle. He fell back into Maryland and built a defensive fort.

The news of Washington's defeat shocked Marylanders. The Maryland Assembly voted to raise money "for his Majesty's use, towards the defence of the colony of Virginia, attacked by the French and Indians."[3] This phrase gave the name "the French and Indian War" to the struggle that followed.

The English sent General Edward Braddock to command a force that would attack Fort Duquesne. The overconfident Braddock,

*General Edward Braddock underestimated the fighting ability of Indians and paid for his error with his life. George Washington (on horseback) takes command as Braddock suffers a mortal wound.*

whose experience was in fighting European wars in the open, dismissed local concerns about the way that he was deploying his troops. The Indians could pose a threat "to your raw American militia," he boasted, "but upon the king's regular and disciplined troops, it is impossible that they should make an impression."[4] After passing through Maryland, Braddock soon found out how wrong he was. His troops were attacked; more than half were wounded or killed. Braddock himself was slain, and only Washington's leadership prevented complete annihilation.

During the next few years, settlers on the frontier lived in constant danger. Once again the rumor arose about Catholics conspiring with the Indians, heightened because most of their French allies were Catholics. Daniel Dulany wrote, "Clamors against Popery are as loud as ever."[5] Catholic landowners found themselves taxed more heavily than Protestants.

Despite early defeats, the British finally assumed the upper hand in combat, and the war ended with a British victory in 1763. As part of the peace settlement, the French turned over millions of square miles of North American territory to the British.

Soon afterward, Charles Mason and Jeremiah Dixon came ashore in Philadelphia. They had been hired—in secret—to finally determine the boundary line between Maryland and Pennsylvania. They worked, often under adverse conditions, for nearly five years. The line they established became known as the Mason-Dixon Line.

One result of their work is the narrowest line-to-line section of any state. With the Potomac River forming a natural border between Maryland on one side and West Virginia and Virginia on the other, at one point near the town of Hancock, Maryland is less than two miles wide. The Amtrak web site observes that because Maryland's border with Pennsylvania is straight, yet its border with West Virginia curves according to the lay of the land, "the engine and tail of our train may be in Maryland, while the middle is in West Virginia!"[6]

"Their great boundary survey was the first, and for many years, the most ambitious, geodetic survey ever conducted," notes surveyor and author Edwin Danson. "It set a precedent for the precise measurement and mapping of vast land distances."[7]

## Charles Mason and Jeremiah Dixon

Astronomer Charles Mason and surveyor Jeremiah Dixon were involved in a 1760 expedition to study the planet Venus. There was considerable public interest in the expedition, and the participants became very well known. In particular, the painstaking, accurate work done by Mason and Dixon attracted favorable attention and made them ideal candidates to solve the difficult Maryland-Pennsylvania border problem.

First the men had to determine the latitude of the southernmost portion of Philadelphia. Then they proceeded due south and set up a "Post mark'd West." Lying at 39 degrees 43 minutes 18.2 seconds north, this marker indicated the precise latitude that the border would follow.

Their next task was to establish the border between Maryland and Delaware. Using observations of a star in Ursa Minor (the "Little Dipper"), they determined the so-called Tangent Line. It ran for more than 80 miles. Their work was so accurate that the line never wavered by more than a few feet from being perfectly straight.

They began their main responsibility—laying out what would later be known as the Mason-Dixon Line separating Maryland and Pennsylvania—in April 1765. They put down a marker every mile and a "crownstone" every five miles. Encased in iron cages, many of these stones can be seen today, with an M on one side and a P on the other. The crownstones also include the Calvert and Penn coats of arms. Mason and Dixon surveyed 233 miles before encountering hostile Indians in 1767 and ending their work. Surveying the remainder of the boundary line was completed eighteen years later.

Mason and Dixon never received any formal honors for their work. Some historians believe that Dixie, a common nickname for the southern United States, came from Dixon's name, because the Mason-Dixon Line is often thought of as the dividing line between free and slave states before the Civil War.

The Mason-Dixon Line

**FYI**
**For Your Information**

George III, painted by Scottish artist Allan Ramsay in 1760. George would rule for sixty years, the second-longest reign in English history. His last years were characterized by mental instability. His son, the future George IV, made most of the important decisions during that time.

Chapter

# Revolution and Statehood

The Mason-Dixon Line was a triumph of peaceful arts. However, by the time Mason and Dixon had completed their work, events had been set in motion that would come to a violent head on the village green at Lexington, Massachusetts.

While the English had won the French and Indian War (allowing Mason and Dixon to begin their work), the conflict put a severe strain on the English treasury. King George III believed that because British soldiers had helped them secure their frontiers, Maryland and the other colonies should pay a portion of the cost of the war.

To raise this money, Parliament passed the Stamp Act in 1765. The act required colonists to place a stamp on many forms of printed matter: newspapers, contracts, even playing cards. It struck especially hard at the wealthier members of the colonies, who were more apt to use paper. They used their power to oppose the act. In Maryland, this opposition took two forms. Daniel Dulany Jr.—the son of the famed landowner and attorney—urged lawful protest. He wrote a pamphlet, *The Consideration on the Propriety of Imposing Taxes in the British Colonies for the Purpose of Raising a Revenue by Act of Parliament,* which argued that the colonists shouldn't be taxed without first giving their consent. It was widely read on both sides of the Atlantic.

At age seventy-one, Thomas Cresap was still full of energy. He hated the Stamp Act as much as he had hated Pennsylvanians. He organized and led a procession that, as reported by Mary Louise Cresap Stevenson, "marched, two and two, taking up the coffin containing the 'Stamp Act' at exactly three o'clock, with drums, and banners, and civic officers, and a figure in a chariot representing the Stamp Agent, and placards containing more truth, than compliments; they marched through the principal streets, and arrived at the gallows, on the Court House green, where the 'Stamp Act' was buried under the gallows."[1]

Other protests were more violent. An angry mob demolished a warehouse belonging to Zachariah Hood, an Annapolis merchant appointed to collect the tax. Another mob burned Hood in effigy. Fearing for his life, the terrified tax collector fled to New York.

Faced with rising opposition, Parliament repealed the Stamp Act the following April. The colonists' relief was short-lived. Parliament soon passed the Townshend Acts, which taxed a number of imported commodities such as tea, glass, paper, and paint. Boston, the most radical city in the colonies, stopped importing these goods and urged the other colonies to join them. Maryland did. In 1770, the British dropped the duties on everything except tea. Maryland relaxed. Events such as the Boston Massacre, in which British troops were said to have gunned down five Boston citizens, passed virtually unnoticed in Maryland.

However, the death of Frederick Calvert, the sixth Baron of Baltimore, in 1771, did cause an uproar. He and his wife didn't get along, so they lived apart and produced no children together. There would be no more Barons of Baltimore. Calvert willed his property rights to Henry Harford, a child he'd fathered out of wedlock. The rush of events would soon deprive Harford, who was only twelve at the time, of his bequest.

In mid-December 1773, a group of patriots thinly disguised as Indians dumped hundreds of chests of tea into Boston Harbor to protest the remaining tea tax. The British imposed a naval blockade on Boston until the colonists there paid for the tea they had destroyed. When the news reached Maryland early in 1774, a recent immigrant to the colony named William Eddis wrote, "I view the impending storm

The Boston Tea Party in late 1773 was one of the decisive events leading to the Revolutionary War. Boston Patriots disguised as Indians dumped hundreds of chests of tea into Boston Harbor. The next year, Maryland had its own protest, in the Annapolis harbor, burning a ship carrying tea.

with inexpressible inquietude."[2] Several months later, he added, "All America is in a flame."[3]

In October, Eddis's words acquired a literal meaning as Maryland staged its own version of the Boston Tea Party. The *Peggy Stewart*, a ship carrying tea, was put to the torch as she lay at anchor in Annapolis harbor. Not all who watched approved. A colonist named John Galloway wrote, "If this is Liberty, if this is Justice, they certainly must have a new code of Laws . . . [this event] makes all men of property reflect with horror on their present Situation; to have their lives and propertys at the disposal and mercy of a Mob is Shocking indeed."[4]

When the news of the opening battles of the Revolutionary War in Massachusetts—Lexington and Concord in April, and Bunker Hill

Samuel Chase, an Annapolis attorney, represented Maryland at the First and Second Continental Congresses. He, Thomas Stone, William Paca, and Charles Carroll of Carrollton signed the Declaration of Independence for Maryland. In 1796, Chase was appointed an associate justice of the Supreme Court of the United States. Although he was impeached in 1804, he was acquitted of any wrongdoing and continued to serve on the Court until his death in 1811.

two months later—reached Maryland, Eddis commented, "In almost every district of this province the majority of the people are actually under arms; almost every hat is decorated with a cockade [badge]; and the churlish fife and drum are the only music of the times."[5]

The colony's leaders lagged behind the populace. When the Second Continental Congress began meeting in 1775, the main topic was independence. As the deliberations extended into the spring of 1776, Maryland was reluctant to take the decisive step. John Adams, who would become the second U.S. president, wrote, "Neither the state of Maryland nor [any] of their delegates were very early in their conviction of the necessity of independence, nor very forward in promoting it."[6] Thomas Jefferson, who would succeed Adams as president, added, "Maryland hung heavily on our backs."[7]

A sense of urgency gripped the Congress in June. Richard Henry Lee of Virginia forced the issue when he introduced a resolution declaring that the political connection between the colonies and Britain "is, and ought to be, totally dissolved."[8] Maryland had two choices: join the other colonies or risk becoming completely isolated.

On June 21, Governor Robert Eden—the brother-in-law of Frederick Calvert—boarded a British ship and left the colony. His departure marked the end of 144 years of proprietary rule in Maryland. One week later, Maryland's delegates to the Congress received instructions from the provincial congress to "concur with the United Colonies, or a majority of them, in declaring the United Colonies free and independent states."[9] On July 2, the colonies took the historic vote to declare their independence.

Four Maryland men signed the Declaration of Independence: Charles Carroll of Carrollton, Samuel Chase, William Paca, and Thomas Stone. While Carroll had a long and distinguished career as a lawyer in Annapolis, he is noted as the only Catholic to sign the Declaration and the last signer to die. His death on November 14, 1832, at the age of ninety-five, brought the Revolutionary era in America to an end.

Although no battles during the war actually took place in Maryland, Chesapeake Bay served as a convenient waterway for both sides to transport troops and equipment. The troops became accustomed to living off the land. They often killed local livestock for food and tore down fences to provide firewood.

Chesapeake Bay—Baltimore in particular—was also important as the home base for privateers, ships officially authorized to capture British merchant vessels. The Continental Navy had only a few ships, and those were generally ineffective. Privateers, on the other hand, were very successful in attacking British shipping. By some estimates, Maryland privateers captured nearly 600 British vessels during the first three years of the war.

Maryland troops also distinguished themselves in battle. George Washington praised the Maryland Line, the colony's regular soldiers, by giving Maryland the nickname of the "Old Line State."

*After Washington crossed the Delaware into Trenton, New Jersey, the tide of the Revolutionary War turned in favor of the colonists. With the war won, and the treaty signed in 1783, the colonies were free to govern themselves as the United States of America. Maryland became the seventh state to ratify the Constitution for the new country.*

With the war over, the Continental Congress met in Annapolis for several months at the end of 1783, making the town the temporary capital of the new United States. George Washington resigned his commission as commander-in-chief there on December 23. Three weeks later, the delegates approved the Treaty of Paris, which officially ended the war.

Meanwhile, to govern their new nation, Maryland and the other states had adopted the Articles of Confederation in 1781. The Articles soon proved far too weak. The first step toward something better was the Annapolis Convention in 1786. Delegates from five states released a report calling for another meeting the following year in Philadelphia. During this Constitutional Convention, fifty-five delegates hammered out what would become the U.S.

Constitution. On April 28, 1788, Maryland became the seventh state to ratify it.

It is perhaps appropriate that Maryland found itself directly in the middle of the thirteen original states of the Union in the order of approval, as it made Father Andrew White somewhat of a prophet. More than 150 years earlier, he had written: "The climate is serene and mild, not oppressively hot like that of Florida and old Virginia, nor bitter cold like that of New England: but preserves, so to speak, a middle temperature between the two, and so enjoys the advantages, and escapes the evils, of each."[10]

This "middle temperature" was also the spirit George Calvert and his successors envisioned for their colony—a place where Catholics and Protestants could live in harmony with each other. As historian John D. Krugler observes, "When it came to political and religious loyalties, the Calverts' vision transcended political thinking. Their model for a new relationship between religious and political institutions ranged too far ahead of their contemporaries."[11]

While this spirit was sometimes squelched, it never completely disappeared from the colony. And there was nothing "middle" about how Marylanders pushed for the adoption of what became the First Amendment to the U.S. Constitution, which reads: "Congress shall make no law respecting an establishment of religion, or prohibiting the free exercise thereof; or abridging the freedom of speech, or of the press; or the right of the people peaceably to assemble, and to petition the Government for a redress of grievances."[12]

Daniel Carroll, the cousin of Charles Carroll, "made the strongest recorded plea for the adoption of the First Amendment," says historian J. Mosswood Ives. Through his efforts, Ives adds, "the spirit of Old Maryland became the spirit of New America."[13]

The First Amendment is one of the cornerstones of the freedom that the United States offers to its citizens. It reflects the convictions that George Calvert hammered out in his mind and conscience in the frozen landscapes of Newfoundland and the courts of English kings nearly four centuries ago.

For Your Information

**1784** The state of Maryland chartered a college, which merged with King William's School to become St. John's College.

**1790** Along with Virginia, Maryland donated land for the District of Columbia, the site of the federal capital of the United States. In 1847, the land that Virginia had provided was returned; the capital is now situated entirely on former Maryland soil.

**1814** During the War of 1812, the British invaded Maryland, burned the Capitol Building and the White House, and then bombarded Fort McHenry near Baltimore. Francis Scott Key, a young Maryland attorney, observed the attack on the fort and wrote the words for "The Star-Spangled Banner."

**1830** The Baltimore and Ohio Railroad offered the first scheduled passenger rail service in the United States, linking Ellicotts' Mills and Baltimore.

**1844** Samuel F.B. Morse sent the first official telegraph message, "What Hath God Wrought," from Washington, D.C., to Baltimore.

**1845** The U.S. Naval Academy opened at Annapolis with 50 midshipmen; today more than 4,000 "middies" attend the Academy.

**1861** Though it permitted slavery, Maryland remained in the Union during the Civil War. Federal troops occupied Annapolis and Baltimore and placed cannons on hills overlooking Baltimore. Rather than facing outward to deter attackers, they were pointed at the city itself to prevent citizen uprisings. Marylanders fought on both sides during the conflict, sometimes facing each other in battle.

**1906** Naval Academy bandmaster Charles Zimmerman and midshipman Alfred Hart Miles composed "Anchors Aweigh," the official song of the U.S. Navy.

**1909** Along with Robert Peary, Maryland resident Matthew Henson became one of the first explorers to stand at the North Pole.

**1967** Thurgood Marshall of Maryland became the first African-American member of the U.S. Supreme Court, where he served for twenty-four years.

**1975** Elizabeth Bayley Seton (1774–1821), founder of the American Sisters of Charity in Emmitsburg, Maryland, became the first American-born saint of the Catholic Church.

Maryland State Flag

# Glossary

**bequest**
**(bee-QWEST)**
something granted to an heir in a will; legacy.

**cockade**
**(kaw-KAYD)**
ornament or decoration worn on a hat.

**executor**
**(ek-ZEH-kyoo-tur)**
a person charged with carrying out the terms of a will.

**geodetic**
**(jee-oh-DEH-tik)**
referring to measurements of the earth's surface that take its curvature into account.

**indentured servants**
**(in-DEN-churd SER-vunts)**
people who are bound to serve another person for a specified period of time in return for costs of their transportation, food, and shelter.

**patron**
**(PAY-trun)**
a person who supports and encourages the development and growth of another person.

**Popery**
**(POH-puh-ree)**
Catholic practices.

**proprietor**
**(proh-PRY-uh-tur)**
a person who owns a colony and has the legal right to make its laws.

**quoit**
**(KWOYT)**
a flat iron or rope ring which is tossed at an upright pin as a game.

**relinquished**
**(ree-LING-kwishd)**
gave up, yielded.

**swashbucklers**
**(SWASH-buk-lurs)**
particularly brave or daring adventurers.

**tenets**
**(TEH-nets)**
beliefs, principles.

**transcended**
**(tran-SEN-dud)**
went beyond normal limits.

**usurp**
**(yoo-SURP)**
overthrow, replace by use of force.

# Chapter Notes

## Chapter 1
## Sailing to "Mary's Land"

1. Andrew White, *Voyage to Maryland* (1633), translated and edited by Barbara Lawatsch-Boomgaarden with Josef IJsewijn (Wauconda, Illinois: Bolchazy-Carducci Publishers, 1995), p. 26.
2. Ibid.
3. Ibid.
4. John D. Krugler, *English and Catholic: The Lords Baltimore in the Seventeenth Century* (Baltimore, Maryland: The Johns Hopkins University Press, 2004), p. 28.
5. Ibid., p. 29.
6. Ted Morgan, *Wilderness at Dawn: The Settling of the North American Continent* (New York: Simon and Schuster, 1993), p. 238.
7. Kugler, p. 101.
8. Thomas O'Brien Hanley, *Their Rights and Liberties: The Beginnings of Religious and Political Freedom in Maryland* (Westminster, Maryland: The Newman Press, 1990), p. 65.
9. Aubrey C. Land, *Colonial Maryland: A History* (Millwood, New York: KTO Press, 1981), p. 8.
10. Ibid., p. 9.
11. White, pp. 34–35.
12. Ibid., p. 37.
13. Ibid., p. 38.

## Chapter 2
## Conflicts Begin

1. Andrew White, *Voyage to Maryland* (1633), translated and edited by Barbara Lawatsch-Boomgaarden with Josef IJsewijn (Wauconda, Illinois: Bolchazy-Carducci Publishers, 1995), p. 26.
2. Robert J. Brugger, *Maryland: A Middle Temperament, 1634–1980* (Baltimore, Maryland:

The Johns Hopkins University Press, 1988), p. 13.

3. Aubrey C. Land, *Colonial Maryland: A History* (Millwood, New York: KTO Press, 1981), p. 34.

4. Thomas O'Brien Hanley, *Their Rights and Liberties: The Beginnings of Religious and Political Freedom in Maryland* (Westminster, Maryland: The Newman Press, 1990), p. 38.

5. Land, p. 50.

6. Ibid., p. 81

7. Lois Green Carr, "Margaret Brent – A Brief History." Maryland State Archives. http://www.msa.md.gov/msa/speccol/ sc3500/sc3520/002100/002177/html/ mbrent2.html

## Chapter 3
## Protestants Come to Power

1. Robert J. Brugger, *Maryland: A Middle Temperament, 1634–1980* (Baltimore, Maryland: The Johns Hopkins University Press, 1988), p. 39.

2. Aubrey C. Land, *Colonial Maryland: A History* (Millwood, New York: KTO Press, 1981), p. 88.

3. Carl Bode, *Maryland: A Bicentennial History* (New York: W.W. Norton, 1978), p. 7.

4. Ibid., p. 9.

## Chapter 4
## Drawing the Line

1. Robert J. Brugger, *Maryland: A Middle Temperament, 1634–1980* (Baltimore, Maryland: The Johns Hopkins University Press, 1988), p. 69.

2. Ted Morgan, *Wilderness at Dawn: The Settling of the North American Continent* (New York: Simon and Schuster, 1993), p. 311.

3. Aubrey C. Land, *Colonial Maryland: A History* (Millwood, New York: KTO Press, 1981), pp. 214–215.

4. Brugger, p. 94.

5. Ibid., p. 95.

6. Amtrak Capitol Limited Route Guide http://www.trainweb.com/routes/route_29/ rg_29.htm

7. Edwin Danson, *Drawing the Line: How Mason and Dixon Surveyed the Most Famous Border in America* (New York: John Wiley & Sons, 2001), pp. 3–4.

## Chapter 5
## Revolution and Statehood

1. *Ohio History*, http://publications.ohiohistory. org/ohstemplate.cfm?action=detail&Page=00 10161.html&StartPage=146&EndPage=164& volume=10&newtitle=Volume%2010%20Pag e%20146

2. Carl Bode, *Maryland: A Bicentennial History* (New York: W.W. Norton, 1978), p. 46.

3. Ibid.

4. Robert J. Brugger, *Maryland: A Middle Temperament, 1634–1980* (Baltimore, Maryland: The Johns Hopkins University Press, 1988), p. 113.

5. Bode, p. 47.

6. Brugger, p. 119.

7. Ibid.

8. Aubrey C. Land, *Colonial Maryland: A History* (Millwood, New York: KTO Press, 1981), p. 313.

9. Ibid. p. 314.

10. Andrew White, "AN ACCOUNT Of the Colony of the Lord Baron of Baltimore, (Cecil, son of the 1st George,) in Maryland, near Virginia: in which the character, quality and state of the Country, and its numerous advantages and sources of wealth are set forth." http://memory.loc.gov/cgi-bin/ query/r?ammem/lhbcb:@field(DOCID+@ lit(lhbcb13427div7))

11. John D. Krugler, *English and Catholic: The Lords Baltimore in the Seventeenth Century* (Baltimore, Maryland: The Johns Hopkins University Press, 2004), p. 249.

12. First Amendment to the United States Constitution http://en.wikipedia.org/wiki/ First_Amendment

13. "Religious Freedom and the Church-State Relationship." Archives of Maryland. http://www.djs.state.md.us/megafile/msa/ speccol/sc2900/sc2908/000001/000138/ html/am138--29.html

# Further Reading

## For Young Adults

Burgan, Michael. *Maryland.* Danbury, Connecticut: Children's Press, 2004.

Doherty, Craig A, and Katherine M. Doherty. *Maryland.* New York: Facts on File, 2005.

Johnston, Joyce. *Maryland.* Minneapoplis, Minnesota: Lerner Publications Company, 2003.

Otfinoski, Steve. *It's My State: Maryland.* New York: Benchmark Books, 2003.

Otis, James. *Calvert of—Maryland A Story of Lord Baltimore's Colony.* Whitefish, Montana: Kessinger Publishing, 2005.

Rauth, Leslie. *Maryland.* New York: Benchmark Books, 2000.

## Works Consulted

Bode, Carl. *Maryland: A Bicentennial History.* New York: W.W. Norton, 1978.

Brugger, Robert J. *Maryland: A Middle Temperament, 1634–1980.* Baltimore, Maryland: The Johns Hopkins University Press, 1988.

Danson, Edwin. *Drawing the Line: How Mason and Dixon Surveyed the Most Famous Border in America.* New York: John Wiley & Sons, 2001.

Hanley, Thomas O'Brien. *Their Rights and Liberties: The Beginnings of Religious and Political Freedom in Maryland.* Westminster, Maryland: The Newman Press, 1990.

Krugler, John D. *English and Catholic: The Lords Baltimore in the Seventeenth Century.* Baltimore, Maryland: The Johns Hopkins University Press, 2004.

Land, Aubrey C. *Colonial Maryland: A History.* Millwood, New York: KTO Press, 1981.

Morgan, Ted. *Wilderness at Dawn: The Settling of the North American Continent.* New York: Simon and Schuster, 1993.

Quinn, Arthur. *A New World: An Epic of Colonial America from the Founding of Jamestown to the Fall of Quebec.* New York: Berkley Books, 1995.

Quinn, David B (editor). *Early Maryland in a Wider World.* Detroit, Michigan: Wayne State University Press, 1982.

Tate, Thad W., and David L. Ammerman (editors). *The Chesapeake in the Seventeenth Century: Essays on Anglo-American Society.* Chapel Hill: The University of North Carolina Press, 1979.

White, Andrew. *Voyage to Maryland (1633).* Translated and edited by Barbara Lawatsch-Boomgaarden with Josef IJsewijn. Wauconda, Illinois: Bolchazy-Carducci Publishers, 1995.

Williamson, Gene. *Chesapeake Conflict.* Westminster, Maryland: Heritage Books, 1995.

## On the Internet

Archives of Maryland Online. "Religious Freedom and the Church-State Relationship." **http://www.djs.state.md.us/megafile/msa/speccol/sc2900/sc2908/000001/000138/html/am138--29.html**

Carr, Lois Green. "Margaret Brent—A Brief History." Maryland State Archives. **http://www.msa.md.gov/msa/speccol/sc3500/sc3520/002100/002177/html/mbrent2.html**

Exploring Maryland's Roots. **http://mdroots.thinkport.org/**

Maryland, the Seventh State **http://www.marylandtheseventhstate.com/index-2.html**

*Ohio History,* Vol. 10, p. 161, "Colonel Thomas Cresap" **http://publications.ohiohistory.org/ohstemplate.cfm?action=detail&Page=0010161.html&StartPage=146&EndPage=164&volume=10&newtitle=Volume%2010%20Page%20146**

St. John's College. "A Brief History of St. John's" **http://www.stjohnscollege.edu/asp/main.aspx?page=1101**

White, Andrew. "*AN ACCOUNT* Of the Colony of the Lord Baron of Baltimore, (Cecil, son of the 1st George,) in Maryland, near Virginia: in which the character, quality and state of the Country, and its numerous advantages and sources of wealth are set forth." **http://memory.loc.gov/cgi-bin/query/r?ammem/lhbcb:@field(DOCID+@lit(lhbcb13427div7))**

# Chronology

**1498** Explorer John Cabot sails along the coast of Maryland.

**1524** Explorer Giovanni da Verrazano passes mouth of Chesapeake Bay.

**1572** Pedro Menendez de Aviles, the Spanish governor of Florida, sails into Chesapeake Bay.

**1608** Captain John Smith, a leader of the Jamestown Colony, explores Chesapeake Bay.

**1621** George Calvert establishes Avalon Colony in Newfoundland.

**1625** George Calvert declares he is a Catholic; King James I names him Baron of Baltimore.

**1629** George Calvert tries to establish a colony in Virginia but is forced to leave.

**1631** William Claiborne establishes first European trading post in Maryland, on Kent Island.

**1632** Cecilius Calvert receives a charter from King Charles I to establish Maryland colony.

**1634** First settlers arrive in Maryland.

**1635** Calvert trading vessels fight what may be first naval battle in American history.

**1645** Richard Ingle captures St. Mary's City, but is forced out late the following year.

**1649** Maryland establishes religious toleration.

**1654** Puritans take over government of Maryland.

**1675** Cecilius Calvert dies. Charles Calvert succeeds him as Lord Baltimore.

**1690** Maryland falls under control of the English crown.

**1694** Annapolis becomes the capital of Maryland.

**1727** First newspaper in the South, the *Maryland Gazette*, begins publication.

**1729** City of Baltimore is founded.

**1754** Maryland becomes involved in the French and Indian War.

**1765** Maryland protests the Stamp Act established by English Parliament.

**1767** Mason-Dixon Line establishes Maryland-Pennsylvania and Maryland-Delaware borders.

**1776** Maryland votes in favor of declaring independence from Great Britain.

**1783** Annapolis becomes temporary capital of the United States and the Treaty of Paris, which ends the Revolutionary War, is signed there.

**1788** Maryland becomes the seventh state of the United States under the terms of the Constitution.

# Timeline in History

**1492**   Christopher Columbus discovers the New World.

**1509**   Henry VIII becomes king of England at the age of eighteen.

**1517**   German clergyman Martin Luther begins the Protestant Reformation.

**1558**   Elizabeth I becomes queen of England and rules for nearly forty-five years.

**1588**   The Spanish Armada attempts to overthrow Queen Elizabeth but fails.

**1607**   Captain John Smith helps found Jamestown Colony in Virginia.

**1608**   Samuel de Champlain founds French settlement in Canada at Quebec.

**1620**   Pilgrims land at Plymouth Bay and found Massachusetts Bay Colony.

**1624**   The Dutch West India Company founds the city of New Amsterdam, which becomes New York City forty years later.

**1630**   Boston, Massachusetts is founded.

**1638**   Swedish settlers found colony of New Sweden.

**1642**   English Civil War begins; it ends four years later with a Puritan victory.

**1660**   The English monarchy is restored as Charles II ascends the throne.

**1664**   English forces capture New Amsterdam and rename it New York.

**1681**   English king Charles II grants Pennsylvania to William Penn.

**1685**   Charles II dies; his brother James II succeeds him.

**1706**   Benjamin Franklin is born in Boston.

**1726**   Jonathan Swift writes *Gulliver's Travels*.

**1732**   George Washington is born.

**1754**   The French and Indian War in North America begins; it ends nine years later with an English victory.

**1773**   Patriots disguised as Indians dump tea into Boston Harbor in what becomes known as the "Boston Tea Party."

**1775**   The Revolutionary War begins with the battles of Lexington and Concord.

**1781**   General George Washington and French allies defeat British General Cornwallis at the Battle of Yorktown, the final battle of the Revolutionary War; the war formally ends two years later.

**1787**   The Constitutional Convention is held in Philadelphia.

**1789**   George Washington becomes the first U.S. president; the French Revolution begins.

**1803**   President Thomas Jefferson completes the Louisiana Purchase from the French, doubling the size of the United States.

**1812**   United States and England fight the War of 1812; it ends late in 1814 with the Treaty of Ghent.

**1826**   Thomas Jefferson and John Adams both die on July 4, the fiftieth anniversary of their signing of the Declaration of Independence.

47

# Index